Surviving! One Man's View of Love, Death, Grief, and ?

Don C. Kittinger

Illustrated by Barbara Rich

VANTAGE PRESS
New York

FIRST EDITION

All rights reserved, including the right of
reproduction in whole or in part in any form.

Copyright © 1993 by Don C. Kittinger

Published by Vantage Press, Inc.
516 West 34th Street, New York, New York 10001

Manufactured in the United States of America
ISBN: 0-533-10311-8

Library of Congress Catalog Card No.: 92-93400

0 9 8 7 6 5 4 3 2 1

CAROL ANN FOX KITTINGER
SEPTEMBER 17, 1935, TO JUNE 16, 1990

THIS BOOK IS DEDICATED
TO MY WIFE, CAROL ANN, WHO
BROUGHT LOVE, CARING, SHARING,
HONESTY, CREATIVITY, AND A ZEST FOR
LIFE INTO OUR THIRTY-FIVE-YEAR
RELATIONSHIP. HER LOVING
MEMORY WILL SUSTAIN ME
AND MAKE THE REST OF
MY LIFE'S PATH A
LITTLE LESS
SCARY.

I may have cancer, but cancer does not have me.
—Carol Ann Fox Kittinger

Contents

Acknowledgments   xi
Introduction   xiii
Prologue   xv

Love   1
Death   25
Grief   39
?   63
Epilogue   83

Artwork created with love and tears.
—Barbara Rich

Acknowledgments

I am deeply indebted to the people who, during this very trying time in my life, made the effort to care, to listen, to give guidance (although I didn't always pay attention), and to allow me to share my life with them and their lives with me. Their compassion, caring, and love were very important and made the difference in my surviving this ordeal.

Gratitude is given to the Hospice personnel, who tended to our emotional needs until Carol Ann's death and to mine afterward. If this book can be used in support of their bereavement counseling, then Carol Ann's memory will live on in an unexpected arena.

A special thanks goes out to Barbara Rich, Carol Ann's and my special friend from Huber Heights, Ohio, who with her great artistic ability provided the illustrations for this book. This gift, with love from a friend, made my efforts a completed work.

Although many family members and friends played an important role in helping to get this book written, reviewed, and finally published, two people were especially helpful: Dr. Mary Kevin Howard Hermann, who became my "intellectual nag," and reintroduced me to my college creative-writing professor, Dr. Virginia Grabill. Dr. Grabill spent an enormous amount of time reviewing my writing to assure that the spelling, punctuation, and grammar were correct. Without these two ladies' support, input, and guidance, this book would not have occurred.

Introduction

This book has been written in hopes that I could reach people who are hurting after a loss of a very special loved one and who might need to know that their loss and pain are not unique or unbearable. I lost my precious wife, Carol Ann, on June 16, 1990, after a seventeen-month ordeal battling liver cancer; my pain after her death was so severe at times that my heart felt that it was going to stop completely. I seriously believed that a person could die of a broken heart, and I was convinced that I couldn't survive the anguish and turmoil of life without her.

Our love had been strong and caring; it had been my anchor and safe harbor for over thirty years. As you read this book, I hope you will come to realize that you can survive, although progress will be slow and some pain will always be present, and that you can continue with your life.

I believe that, because of what my marriage and life with Carol Ann gave me, it is possible to share my life and love with someone else, *someday*. I miss my wife, I feel cheated by her death, I suffer because of my loss; but I also know Carol Ann would demand that I look forward, let my memories sustain me, learn to live again, reach out to others, and fully expect to love and be loved again, *someday*.

After Creation

As the sun rose from the depths of night,
And bathed the day in brilliant light,
I rubbed my eyes and looked at the words
That had come from my pen like flying birds;
I smiled, feeling no tiredness,
And no need to stop for rest.

Carefully consulting each past-composed note,
I thought, emoted, and wrote,
Letting each sentence grow freely,
Like limbs on a tree.

Even though the technicalities may not be right,
And my spelling is really a fright,
And even though my writings cross no sea,
Satisfied I will be,
Because, whether or not I'm a genius of a sort,
My creating comes from my soul and heart.

My creating has given words to the world,
Arriving like banners unfurled,
And if read by people who are free,
I hope they understand this is a part of me.

Prologue

To understand my essays and poetry, one needs a certain amount of background information about Carol Ann and me.

We met in August 1955, just before I started college in September. Our meeting was sort of arranged by two of her friends, who thought we might like each other. Naturally, after the big buildup we both received before our first encounter, we didn't hit it off right away. After we recovered from the pushing of our mutual friends, we discovered that they had something: we did have a lot in common. We both enjoyed dancing, playing cards, bowling, and going to movies. Our common ties included a strong church and family background and a love of art. Even our families had crossed each other's paths. Her father and my mother had worked at the telephone company at the same time. My cousin and Carol Ann were in the same confirmation class. I had even worked as a busboy in a restaurant that her father ate in.

After I graduated in June 1960 and started my civilian Air Force career at Wright-Patterson Air Force Base in Ohio, we were married on September 3, 1960. Our marriage was not too much different from most couples'. We had to learn to give and help each other to grow in our marriage. Although we had no children of our own, our house was always filled with neighbors' children, many music students, and friends' children, who would emotionally adopt us as their second parents. Carol Ann was a veritable Pied Piper of the neighborhood. As most couples do experience some difficulties in marriage, we had minor inconveniences as we both tried to be true to our individual selves while still assuring that our marriage always took top priority.

Our life together arrived at my retirement time in April 1988, with great hopes and plans for returning to our hometown of Evansville, Indiana, to build our dream retirement home. Carol Ann was going to teach, and I was going to concentrate on my art work. We both enjoyed travel, and we would be able to go when we wanted to and still have a firm anchor established to return to in Indiana. Our home was started in June 1988; we moved in the week before Thanksgiving and started finishing the inside.

On January 7, 1989, Carol Ann found a large growth in her abdomen, and we went to one of the local hospitals immediately. After a week of tests and exploratory surgery, it was necessary to start Carol Ann on chemo treatments to try to arrest the liver cancer. After six months of treatments, which included very terrible side effects, Carol Ann's cancer was declared in remission in July 1989. We thought we had won a very wonderful reprieve for years of life together. During this time of high hopes for Carol Ann's recovery, we had a blow to our thankfulness when my eighty-six-year-old father died in August 1989. On top of this, Carol Ann's father had died in 1987. While we were trying to recover from my father's death, Carol Ann discovered the return of the tumor in October 1989. This was even harder to accept than when we first found the tumor—especially since the monthly checks at the cancer center in August and September had shown no signs of the tumor.

After several more attempts at treating the cancer, Carol Ann and I decided, in February 1990, that enough was enough. We wanted to have whatever life she had left to be free of doctors, nurses, needles, chemo treatment side effects, feeling like a guinea pig, being apart while she was in the hospital, and the swings of emotions between hope and despair. I took her home from the hospital, cared for her, loved her even more because of her quiet strong dignity, and watched the love of my life slowly and painfully disintegrate before my eyes; until on June 16, 1990, she left me for a place where she would never have to suffer anymore. Now it was my time for despair, suffering, anger, grief, and the worst pain I have faced in my life.

Pain

The pain is always there,
But old and new friends help
As time pushes me to the future,
It changes the hurt from stabbing to dull.

The simple joyful things,
Still start the tears flowing;
Good memories try to cover the thoughts of her pain,
But at times I still see her terrible struggle.

Pain, you are at times my most severe enemy;
Pain, at other times you are my dull, constant companion;
Pain, you make me realize I am alive;
Pain, you will not win!

Surviving! One Man's View of Love, Death, Grief, and ?

Love

Love is difficult to explain. Actually, love needs to be experienced, and even then it is not easily explained. There are of course many stimuli that affect two people in love. Sharing, caring, honesty, giving without expecting anything in return, confidence in the fidelity of the relationship, and being together while still allowing the other person his/her own identity are some of the things that affect a growing and healthy relationship. Eventually the close and special act of expressing that love with the intimacy of the physical joining of two bodies can only strengthen that love and give each a chance to be completely immersed in the emotional and physical joy that two people can share.

The sharing of two lives at the beginning of marriage is so full of promise and the expectations are so very high that we wonder what will really happen. Although many people say that a successful marriage takes work, I believe that what it takes is both remembering the other is one's best friend, especially after the rush of physical attraction and the thrill of intimate relations have calmed somewhat.

Carol Ann and I were very lucky, since we were the best of friends very early in our relationship. All through our dating, courtship, and married life together, we easily shared, discussed things that concerned us, gave space to each other when required, and were able to grow closer together each year. We also easily did little things that showed how we felt about each other. The inexpensive little presents for no particular reason, the daily hugs, the greeting card just to say we knew what we had was special, or the phone call to ask for a "date" even though married did wonders to enhance our individual self-esteem. When two people truly like themselves, recognize their own identity, and are not afraid of honesty, their merging into a commitment can only be best for both of them. I know that we were very fortunate in having this. That's why I miss her so much that at times it's hard to believe I will really survive. But what we had also makes me hope I can maybe find it again.

Whenever I have heard the question of "When did you know that you loved Carol Ann?" I smile and remember that night in 1956. We had been dating since August 1955, and I recall that at Thanksgiving of 1956 she was still just a date. After one of our dates, we went through our goodnight ritual: Carol Ann would stand in the front window of her parents' home and watch as I went around the car. I would wave, she would wave, I would get into the car and drive away. Well, this one night was I ever surprised when I got in my car! I had no steering wheel, no brake pedal, no gas pedal, and in fact no dashboard. I had actually gotten into the back seat and had even shut the door. I sat there completely in shock by my action. I finally realized that if she affected me this much I was lost to the single life. I knew I might as well let her know that she was the only one for me and I wanted to spend the rest of my life with her. Besides, if I were going to try to drive from the back seat, I had better have a partner to sit in the front or at least to tell me where the front seat was!

Comes Manhood
(Written November 1956)

How little I knew of me,
How much there was to learn,
My innermost thoughts were on a rough sea,
All I needed to be was a little stern.

To take a look is what I needed,
The voice of the real me
Is what I needed to have heeded,
And then, I would have been surprised to see.

To come face to face with reality,
As all men should at some time,
Then, like a new dawning, it happened to me.
What is life without something to keep you in line?

To learn the truth about people,
Is what I needed most of all,
Like a shining light from a high steeple,
Came the call.

Came the call from the depths of my soul:
"Let me help you,"
And as if I had been put on the roll,
Towards something great and new.

My life now had meaning and a path to travel,
At last I had found the happiness key,
It came at first as soft as a brook's babble,
And then shouting from the highest tree.

All the compassion I never knew I had
Came bursting forth and made me stand,
Not as the same selfish lad,
But at last a man.

From August 1955, until December 1956, we had dated other people. In November 1956, I realized she wasn't just a date but the one person I wanted to spend the rest of my life with. A couple of weeks before Christmas, I declared my intentions, and they were received favorably. Unfortunately, a week later, Carol Ann realized that I meant that I wanted to go steady, get engaged, and get married as soon as I finished college. She thought I had meant "let's go STEADY." Carol Ann called off our very short time of going steady.

We separated, but of course we still went to the same church and attended the same Sunday school class. We also ran around in the same crowd, went to the same dances, parties, and picnics (Carol Ann with her date and I with mine). When we had stopped dating, I told Carol Ann that my feelings for her weren't going to change; and, when she was ready for an absolute commitment and wanted back, she should call me.

Without Her Love
(Written Spring 1957)

What would life be without someone who cares?
It would be the same
As if someone took the color from the sunset
Or removed the rainbow after the rain.

And so we must admit
That life without love
Is the game we all would want to quit
Because we would have enough
Of nobody to care about,
So we all agree
That, no matter how stout,
Or strong a man may be.

Love's sweet gentle breezes
Will bring forth his most tender feelings,
And like a buzzing of a thousand bees,
His mind will go reeling.

Until he wonders what is wrong,
And then, like a crash
Of a large gong,
His heart will know in a flash,
That she is not just a date
But the girl brought
To him by fate,
And he finds what he thought he had not sought.

Love has come and changed this man
And made him desire,
Not only among the great men to stand
But to rise above the highest tower,
And succeed for her sake,
To deserve her love
As shining as a sunset on a lake
Because life would be nothing without her love.

Loved and Lost
(Written Spring 1957)

What is the best way to say I care?
How can I let her know?
Should I lay my soul bare,
When I know that her feelings for me are just so-so?

Should I tell her what I feel—
That down in my heart
I know that for her my love is real?
I thought I was so smart
And couldn't fall in love
As each day goes by, I can tell a little more
That I didn't need a shove
To find love's door.

Is it wise to confess
How much she really means to me
And that she is the best
Of everything to me?

How can I tell her that she is the one
I want to be my wife—
Not one, but a thousand and one
Years of my life?
Each memory of her stays in my mind—
How she is so sweet,
Wonderful, and kind,
How to hear her voice is a real treat.

I remember so well
That first sweet kiss
And how I knew I'd like to dwell
Forever with this sweet young miss.

But, alas, how can a lowly knave like me
Expect a lovely queen
Like her to be
Not just in my dream,
But spending her life loving me
As much as I love her?
But now I must pay the fee,
And now one more mister
Has loved and lost.
But, whatever it will be,
I will gladly pay the cost, just to keep her in my memory.

    During the time Carol Ann and I weren't dating, she started dating a man named Mark McDaniels.* Although I didn't know

* Fictitious name

him, I heard his name quite often in connection with Carol Ann. One Tuesday night at the weekly dance at the YWCA, a group of guys were standing in the hallway planning the next weekend's picnic. One of my friends asked me if I knew whom Carol Ann would be going with, and I replied, "Oh, I guess some creep named Mark McDaniels." As this group of guys went back into the dance, a guy I didn't know came over and said, "Don, I just wanted to introduce myself. I am Mark McDaniels." Needless to say, my face got a little red.

That weekend, on the way back from the picnic, Carol Ann was in Mark's car and I was in my car with my date. As we approached Chandler, Indiana, I remembered the cop who sat at the main crossroad in his car and tried to catch speeders. Unfortunately, the cop usually dozed off and wasn't very good at catching anybody. Well, being a little green-eyed about Mark, I taunted him into driving a little too fast through Chandler. Just before the cop's favorite intersection, I sped up, blew my horn, and the cop woke up just in time to catch Mark, who did get a traffic ticket. Although not really liking myself for what I had done, I did get a momentary rush of satisfaction. I guess love makes a person do strange things.

Easter '57
(Written Spring 1957)

Although I had planned to spend
This Easter going steady with you,
It seems that the trend
Is not towards what I want to do.

So, instead of sending myself today,
I send these flowers
Though they may
Last only a few hours.

Please wear them this Easter Sunday;
Wear them and remember this lad;
Remember only if the memories are gay,
And forget them if they are sad.

For whatever will be
In your future or mine,
I only want to see
You find happiness for all time.

    Since I was convinced that each of us was the best the other could find, I was positive that Carol Ann would tell me that we should get back together. Just about six months after we stopped dating, my sister came to visit. Pat had loved Carol Ann from the first and wanted her to come to supper. Since I wasn't angry with Carol Ann, I agreed to pick her up and take her home. When we had been dating, we would go dancing just about every Saturday night. The night that Carol Ann came to supper was a Saturday, and on the way back to her house, she said, "Don, can we go dancing?" I stopped the car, looked at her smiling face, and asked, "Are you trying to tell me something?" Her smile grew even bigger, and she said, "Yes, I want back for life." Although it was the 22nd of June, the sky lit up like the 4th of July and we celebrated that day every month for almost thirty-three years.

Return '57
(Written July 1957)

What ecstasy is the first kiss of returning sweethearts!
What a sublime feeling occurs
When they return after being apart!
Once again love has been found to endure.

The sunshine has finally returned to the cloudiest day,
The sweet fragrance of the love flower is again present,
And they know that love will stay and stay,
For always and not for a time to rent.

The clock ceases its running,
She is queen and he is king,
And time has no meaning,
Because the sweet kisses take away the sting.

Take away the sting of the lonely nights,
When at times they suffered such pain,
They would have put up such fights,
Just to be together again.

But, how can they enjoy the warmth
Of love's sweet gentle breeze,
Unless they have suffered and felt the storm
Of loneliness and defeat?

The important thing is not how or why they fell,
But how they reshape their lives together,
And come from the loneliness of hell
Back to the heaven of love for each other.

When I think about what Carol Ann did for me in our thirty-five-year relationship, I remember a letter my sister, Pat, sent during Carol Ann's battle against cancer. I had received a phone call from Pat telling me that there was a phrase in a letter that Carol Ann was going to receive that really didn't say what she wanted to say.

The letter was telling Carol Ann how much Pat appreciated her as a sister-in-law, how much Carol Ann was loved, how much Pat was aware that we had done a lot for each other, and how much Pat knew that when Carol Ann met me I was a "social misfit." Pat told me after she sent the letter she knew she really wanted to say that I was a "diamond in the rough," and she didn't want me to be angry about what was in the letter.

I still smile when I think about that phone call and letter, because my sister was so very accurate about what she had said. My life, after meeting Carol Ann, took on substance, meaning, and love. My rough edges did get smoothed with a lot of tender loving care. Although I kiddingly told my sister that I was very angry and wouldn't talk to her ever again, we still laugh about the "social misfit" letter.

Season's Greeting to the One I Love
(Christmas message from Carol Ann to Don in 1957)

Sweetheart, to me you've always been
    The very sweetest part
Of all the precious hopes and dreams
    I have within my heart.

You've brought the deepest happiness
    That I have ever known,
Sweetheart, that's why my love belongs
    To you, and you alone.

Merry Christmas

A Poem?
(Written February 1958)

Although I am not a poet,
For I know not how to rhyme,
And this will surely show it,
But if you would be the valentine of mine.

I could make verse,
Day in and day out,
With its probably not getting much worse,
Than this, no doubt.

For if you say yes
And give your heart to me
And seal the bargain with a kiss,
I will probably buzz like a bee.

To be or not to be,
Where this line
Came from I cannot see,
Except to end this rhyme with
Be my valentine.

All My Love
(Given to Carol Ann on our wedding day in 1960)

As time swiftly floats by
And the hour of our joining comes near,
A present for you I wanted to buy,
A special present for the one most dear.

What should I give? I can't find any rules.
What to give? I can't ask any elf.
I can't give you mansions, riches, or jewels,
So I give what I can—my love and myself.

So as we join hands, minds, and love,
Smile and be happy, pretty one,
For I freely give you all my love,
To last till eternity is done.

I Love You
(Valentine message from Carol Ann to Don in 1987)

I love you because:
    you smile, go swimming with me, hold hands,
        drive carefully, kiss me in the A.M., like lazybear,
            come home for lunch, hold hands, build greenhouses,
                open my car door, go out to eat at Friendly's,
                    kiss me at noon, and because
                        you like me as I am.

The Quiet Times

    I think the quiet times, especially the warm fuzzy ones, were the most comforting. But they are also the most painful to remember. The way she would pull her legs up on the couch while she quietly contemplated her next move in the Scrabble game brings a warm, gentle feeling to my well-being. But then the realization that I will never see that again brings a cold chill to my soul.
    I remember the many times when she was playing the piano, organ, or harp or when she was teaching one of her many students, and I would marvel at her quiet self-confidence. She was such a gentle but still such a strong person that it amazed people. Little did

I know that this quiet unassuming strength would sustain me through the most difficult time I would experience in my life. Without her example, especially during her very deep pain, I could not have been as strong as I was nor would I have been able to go on without her.

I miss the love, the sharing, the growing, and most of all the simple quiet times. The crunch of the leaves during the walks through the woods will never be the same, but the memories do help me to reach out to new friends and try to experience whatever life has to offer. I will stumble, skin my emotions, pick myself up, reach out again, and stumble again. But because of those many special quiet times
>   I can survive,
>   I can feel,
>   I can live,
>   and someday I may love again.

Without Her

Can I ever again watch a sunset?
Can I ever feel joy?
Can I ever speak the pain of my loneliness?
How can I survive without her?

Can I share the depth of my suffering?
Can I let my friends see my grief?
Can I face my uncertain future?
How can I survive without her?

Can I celebrate the holidays?
Can I give and receive happy greetings?
Can I really go on with life?
How can I survive without her?

I can try, because she is still with me,
To reach out because she is still with me,
To help others understand because she is still with me.
I can survive without her
    But not without pain,
      Not without help,
        Not without love.

Therefore, I reach out,
    give compassion where needed,
      share friendship when I can,
        give hugs if wanted,
          and hope that by sharing the love that she gave to me
          I can someday be loved in return.

To My Love at Christmas

Although you are gone,
I still see your anticipation,
Hear your beautiful music,
Feel your quiet presence.

Although you are gone,
I still see your joy,
Hear your guidance,
Feel your tender touch.

Although you are gone,
I still see your smiling face,
Hear your laughter,
Feel your special love.

Although you are gone,
    You are not really gone,
      You are in my soul,
        And in my heart,
          Because you are my love.

Sleep

Sleep,
Will you ignore me again tonight?
Can I make it without you?
I toss, I turn, and I fail once more.

Sleep,
Maybe you are not necessary,
But my body cries out for you to arrive
While my mind pushes you away once more.

Sleep,
The ticking clock counts the passing minutes
While the furnace continually cycles on and off.
What must I do to find you?

Sleep,
The place where you should be is empty,
And I can't accept that you won't return,
While I know I must.

Sleep,
    Take away my memories of your pain.
Sleep,
    Give me some peace for a little while.
Sleep,
    Let me remember the good times.

Sleep,
    I need you,
        I must have you,
            I can't survive without you.

To Share Again

My heart is broken but mending.
The why of the loss of my love is unanswerable;
The joys we shared will always be mine,
While the void left may be carefully filled again.

Your caring ways taught me well.
I am trying to understand your wisdom;
I know you don't want me to be alone;
Your advice will be my standard.

My mind tells me what to do
While my emotions scream no;
You left a special love in my care,
And with your guidance,
    I may be able to share it again.

Valentine's Day

Why must one day hurt more than another?
I can't possibly miss her more today than yesterday!
February 14 is just a date on the calendar,
But it is known as the day of sweethearts.

My first and I thought only love is gone.
My emotions can't accept a substitute right now.
I hope time will make a difference
And this special love may be felt again.

Red and White

The red and white shine against each other
Like a merging of two large fireworks displays,
The sharpness of their colors
Magnify the loss I have suffered.

Vivid colors remind me how much we shared
And how much more I have left to give,
What you left me with
I will nurture.

Memories

Memories are stored in the crevices of my mind
To be retrieved when needed,
They are always mine and always special
And can pull me through the current crisis.

Memories of that special smile
Bring joy to my heart;
The lasting glow from the quiet times
Still warm my very soul.

Memories sustain me,
Give me a strong foundation to build on!
Memories remind me what made me what I am
And allow me to go on to whatever I will be.

Once Again

My mind and heart see her clearly;
It still seems that she will return tomorrow;
My loss must be just a nightmare
And will vanish when I really open my eyes.

This feeling of frustration has to go away;
I constantly compare my past to my present,
And I know that this is a useless task
Because it does no good.

My life must be in the present and future;
Although I will always be tied to my past,
What I am is primarily because of her,
And in that I must rejoice.

As the pain lessens,
And as the new stage in my life emerges,
I must learn to enjoy each day,
Plan ahead,
    And most of all be open to love once again.

Because of Her

Future events await me;
New friendships are out there;
Anticipation about tomorrow excites me;
While today's joy sustains me.

I have not and cannot ever forget her,
And I miss her gentle touch very much;
Her last guidance to me was to live,
Enjoy each day, and not be alone.

She comforts me in my grief,
Rejoices when I am happy,
Consoles me and drives away the fog
While telling me that things will get better.

Because of her I will survive,
   I may enjoy life again,
     I hope to be complete again,
       And I know that the capability to be special for
         somebody, someday, will return.

It Is Time

The time arrived before I was ready;
Morning stillness was broken.
What an ominous noise the truck made!
Piano and organ were extensions of her;
When she left they too seemed to wither.

To not be played would be such a waste;
They must make music again.
Letting go is difficult,
But seeing them not being used is worse;
It is time to make the right decision.

To know that their music will bring someone a smile
Or that someone will learn from her teaching tools
Will make the parting easier;
I can't possibly regret that, as much as I miss her music;
She is gone, and seeing them every day hurts too much.

It is time to close one more wound,
To take one more healing step,
Although just a piano and organ,
They were necessary for her creative soul,
And maybe when they are used again, there will be
    a little more peace for both of us.

Harp and Dulcimer

Harp and dulcimer
Carol Ann and music,
The notes must fill the air again;
These two musical instruments must be played.

I must choose carefully;
The right person must have them.
What criteria do I use?
Love of Carol Ann and music are important.

The key has to be Carol Ann's wishes,
She would choose family first,
And that must be my guidance.
Therefore, the harp and dulcimer go to the Foxes.

Easter '91

It is so hard not to be sad,
Even though this special day's happiness surrounds me,
Everywhere there are couples and families,
While I have my loved one only in my memory.

We had so much more we planned on sharing.
She was taken away from me.
Now I feel cheated,
And it's unfair.

The pain returns;
The tears flow,
While anguish tries to cover me.
I wonder if it will ever really get better.

Time is supposed to be the answer,
But how can I get to my future
When the present hurts so very much
And my best efforts cause more pain?

I know I must rejoice in what we had
And realize that the pain will subside again
Because her special love will always be with me
And sustain me.

Life Does Go On

Today plans were made for Carol Ann's last musical instrument.
Her thirty-six-year-old piano needs to be played.
Her wish was for it to go to Julie.
Therefore, I called the mover.

One more change to make it easier for me, and
I can't watch the piano not being used anymore.
As I sit here making arrangements,
My thoughts are about the outside environment.

The air has turned cold,
Steam rises from the ponds,
An early winter blast roared in last night,
While this morning, snow gently fell.

Although I'm not ready,
The season must change.
Trees and plants need to go dormant,
Rest, survive the winter, and wait for spring.

Each year nature's cycles return,
Changes occur,
Some things don't survive, but
Life does go on.

Death

When we discuss death in the abstract, it is easy to understand that it is actually just a part of the cycle of life. In experiencing real life, I find it isn't that easy to be objective. We are all going to experience loss of friends and loved ones during our lifetime, and I hope by sharing my feelings I will help you resolve the emotional conflicts that you will have to face. Although we can—at least try to—come to grips with our feelings about death, I guess nobody is ever really ready or prepared when the very special love of his/her life is taken away. What is even more difficult is to see the person one has shared everything of importance with waste away from cancer before his/her eyes. To watch the love of my life disintegrate from a vibrant, giving, loving, sharing lady to a pain-racked shell of her former self was so devastating that I felt that I must surely die from my own pain.

Why?

We met,
    We cared,
        We shared,
           We grew,
                We loved.
Then, against our desires,
    She left.

Now,
>   I suffer,
>   I cry,
>   But, I do survive.
Why?
>   Because I have loved.

Everything that the medical profession tries gives hope, and then the insidious cancer rears its terrible destructive power again and slams you down into deep despair. Even a very strong belief in God is tested severely. You pray and pray and eventually try to make a pact with God to save her. I know that I offered to exchange my life for hers. I just couldn't believe that such a talented, loving, sharing person as Carol Ann could possibly be leaving this world. Her work here could not have been completed at the young age of fifty-five.

Why Her?

She had much talent;
Her caring ways reached many;
Her giving touched lives.
Why her?

Was her mission in life really complete?
As a teacher, she was special;
As a friend, she was irreplaceable.
Why her?

As a daughter, sister, aunt, and wife, she was the best.
What will we do without her?
Where is her essence now?
Why her?

Where is her creativity, love, and spirit?
It must be in everybody she touched.
"Why her?" cannot be answered,
I can only rejoice in what we had and reach out to share the special love she left in my care.

Even though Carol Ann was suffering terribly, she constantly worried about me and how I would survive. She was trying to make sure I knew how to cook and how to do other household chores she had always done. Although I didn't know it at the time and in fact didn't find out about it from my sister until November 1990, Carol Ann was trying to make sure that there were single ladies in the groups that visited her. Carol Ann told my sister she wanted me to realize there were single ladies out there and she didn't want me to be alone after she died. I should have caught on the day Carol Ann wanted to discuss when I would start seeing women and bringing them to the house. I told her I didn't want to talk about it since I knew I wouldn't be interested and wouldn't ever want to try to find somebody else. Again, I guess Carol Ann knew me better than I did.

Anyway, she insisted that I listen when she said I should be very careful when I started bringing ladies to the house because there might be someone out there that would take one look at our dream house and do anything to move in permanently. I couldn't believe she was giving me advice about when I started to date. But I should have, since she was very logical, very optimistic, and always thinking about the other person's welfare. She wanted the best for everybody—especially me. But to feel that way even if she couldn't be there to enjoy the friendship or the thrill of a new experience was hard for me to understand. But it has carried over and helps me to survive.

During this very trying time, there were still moments of very special tender happenings that I stored in my memories. After Carol Ann got so sick, I naturally took over the household chores and we jokingly called those duties SUZY work. One night one of our special friends, Vi, was visiting and planning to sit with Carol Ann so I could get some sleep. The three of us were talking and reminiscing, and I said, "I guess SUZY should get busy and do the laundry." Vi looked perplexed and asked, "Who is SUZY?" Carol Ann got the biggest smile and said, "That's Don." I imagine that I will always remember that beautiful special smile.

As Carol Ann lost more and more weight, her rings wouldn't stay on. She was very concerned about losing them. One Sunday after we had been out shopping on Friday night, she realized her wedding ring was not on her finger. We couldn't find it. We practically tore the house apart, looking under all the furniture, behind cushions, in every drawer, and in every possible place that she could have put it. Carol Ann was sure she had the ring on in the house after we had been shopping, but we called all the stores anyway without any luck. As each day passed and the more I looked and didn't find it, Carol Ann got more distraught and frantic about not wearing her wedding ring.

I finally called Vi and asked her to stop at a jewelry store on the way out for her next visit and pick up a ring that was something of a facsimile to Carol Ann's ring (I didn't leave the house without her). When Vi brought the ring, Sophie—one of the Hospice workers—was here taking care of Carol Ann. Using Sophie and Vi as semi-official witnesses, I gave Carol Ann the new ring and told her that we just got remarried as we had planned to do on our thirtieth anniversary. Carol Ann looked at me, broke out in her impish smile, and said, "If I just got married, I need a kiss." Needless to say between Sophie, Vi, and me, a few tears fell. Having the new ring eased Carol Ann's anguish and calmed her.

After Carol Ann died and just before the funeral, I was going through the list of jewelry that she wanted to give to family and friends, and in her jewelry box wrapped inside one of her necklaces was her wedding ring. I can only imagine that Carol Ann was so worried about losing it that without my knowledge she had got out of bed and stored her ring for safekeeping and then forgotten that she had. At least I found it in time to place it on her finger before her funeral.

Once I really accepted the fact that she was going to die, I really began to have problems dealing with my emotions. I didn't want her to suffer anymore, but the eternal hope that she somehow could survive pushed me to want one more week, one more day, one more hour. As Carol Ann's pain became worse and she lost more and more weight, she began to ask me to help her die. I wanted to hold on to her, but how could I when it meant such pain? I was so concerned that she would find some way that I did not leave her alone once the last five weeks. If it had not been for my friends, my family, and the people from Hospice filling in when I needed sleep, I am convinced I might have died myself—but God did not grant my prayer that we might go together.

Along with all the churning emotions I was experiencing, there was always guilt associated with almost all the decisions made in trying to fight cancer. Did we have the right doctor? Did we pick the right treatment? Did we go to the best facility available? Although trying to second-guess is obviously counterproductive, I have found others do it too. In our situation my biggest regret was convincing Carol Ann to go back into chemo treatment one more time. In January 1990, she had decided to let happen whatever would happen. The treatments were making her very sick, and the one time of remission had lasted only four months, which was not worth the side effects and the deep despair of having our hopes dashed again. Although we had discussed not going back into treatment, and even though I had agreed with Carol Ann's decision, when our cancer doctor told us about a different chemo treatment that had not been making the patients sick, I convinced Carol Ann to try it for me. I still just couldn't imagine living without her. I guess all of us are really very selfish.

Although dreading the very thought of the hospital, the IVs, and the possible side effects, she agreed. Unfortunately, the treatment made Carol Ann extremely sick. From that point in February

1990, she got sicker, lost weight, got sicker, lost more weight, and had worse and worse pain. Even though I know that the cancer would have taken her from me anyway, I still suffer from my decision that she try chemo treatment one more time. Although I know that I am being unrealistic, I feel that I deserted her for the first time in our lives, and the nightmares come back. Of course I realize that—if I hadn't wanted to try—I would be regretting that decision also. It is so devastating and difficult to understand that the chemicals that kill the cancer cells also kill the very cells that sustain your loved one's life.

Someday

When she died,
A part of me did too,
As they buried her,
They covered part of me with the dark dirt.

The loss of the love of my life,
Caused the loss of part of my emotions,
The slow healing process may rejuvenate my ability to
   care.
Until I am whole again, I must be careful.

Although I know it is too soon,
The desire to make some commitment is very strong,
To receive complete love could be easy,
But without return it could destroy both of us.

My hurting emotions cry out for what I had,
While my intellect tries to control those emotions.
I must use time as my ally
And not rush so that I am my own worst enemy.

Just as a swimmer at times must tread water,
Emotionally I need to just stay afloat;
I must allow what time I need to recover,
So that someday I can honestly and completely say I care,
Oh yes, someday.

I don't claim to have any great wisdom about what one should do or not do to prolong a person's life, but I have decided I do realize the way I intellectually feel about what happened with our situation. I do know that whatever decision a person makes at a given time with the facts available at that time has to be the best one. I have been trying very hard not to beat myself up by second-guessing, but I am smart enough to understand that it is normal to do so, and I must learn to just believe that I did the best I knew to do and accept that what I did was therefore right and was the only thing I could have done. I am slowly learning, and generally speaking, I am O.K.—most of the time.

A Brief Moment in Time

It is a typical early fall day. The air is turning a little cooler, and the trees are just starting to change from the deep lush green to small patches of orange and red. All the signs remind me that the warm days of summer are once again a part of my memories and that my future holds some cold, dreary winter days. Fall, that transition from the carefree joy of summer to the dark and cold winter, will give me time to remember and reflect upon the love and friendships I shared in the brilliant, hot summer sun—experiences that seemed as if they would never end are really only a brief moment in time.

As the sun sinks behind the tree line, the evening sounds change the surrounding atmosphere and force my mind to become acutely aware that things do change and plans formed yesterday

may not be valid today. As the night becomes darker and the night winds chase away the cloud cover to encompass somebody else's life, the long silvery moonlight shows the night as not being scary or full of unknown situations. There are still the pockets of extremely dark uncertain areas of the forest that someday have to be faced and, if not conquered, at least recognized as solvable.

The creatures of the night start to appear. The hoot of the large owl sounds from far away and then increases as this night creature makes its territorial rounds. The swishing of its wings reminds me how quietly in the end she finally left this mortal life. My reason for life had been taken away, just as sure as the darkness of the night takes away the brilliant hot rays of the daytime sun. I know that this deep, empty, painful void can never be completely filled or that the complete love we had for each other can never be felt with any other person in the same way. I also know that what we had can only help me survive the many cold winter nights until someday the warmth of the spring starts to melt the icy grip of pain, anger, and loneliness.

As I sit here and watch the two beautiful deer slowly walk through the woods passing from the darkness of the big old trees into the bright light of the silvery moon, I realize that the cycle of life, love, joy, pain, pleasures, and even death are just brief moments and are what make us what we are today. The sum of all these experiences must sustain me and help me go on with whatever is in my uncertain future.

Storms

Black clouds cover the horizon,
As the storm brews and stirs the countryside.
Where does this violent upheaval get its strength?
How long will the siege last?

Brilliant flashes of lightning cover the darkened sky.
Where is this energy directed?
As the strong wind roars its anger,
The destruction is widespread and random.

Angry billows of dust and debris roll across the valleys,
Slam into the hills, and settle into mounds of spent energy.
What will arise from the stacks of devastation?
Where will the push for revitalization come from?

To rebuild after the storm is possible, but difficult,
The rejoining of separated anchors is required,
And fractured support cables need to be rewoven,
But the process, at best, is painfully slow.

Internal stress needs to be defined;
External results need to be repaired;
Side effects take their toll
While the enormous pressures build and build.

Realization finally settles in:
The storm is from within,
Dark clouds are really my very personal anger,
Anger at the situation I am in,
Anger at the medical profession for not being good enough,
Anger at what other people have and I don't any more,
Anger at myself for being so angry.
Anger has boiled for months and pushes me unmercifully,
Anger, just one more emotion to contend with while recovering.

To Search for an Answer

Whenever I look back at the frantic times,
I wonder how I really survived.
What was the driving force that made me go on?
Why did I try so hard?
One reason must have been to search for an answer.

Her life was cut too short, and
I knew that I couldn't survive without her love.
As the pain rolled in and out and covered my existence,
I felt as if I was drowning, and
Sometimes I just wanted to quit.

There was no rhyme or reason for her death since
She had so much more to give.
The people dear to her needed her more, and
I wondered why should I go on.
One reason must have been to search for an answer.

Although my intellect told me to go on,
My emotions cried out to stop the pain,
Shut off my brain, and not to look to the future.
Passage of time has hardened the scars, but
Memories can overpower me and wounds are opened again.

Each time the pain returns for a visit,
I remember to rejoice in what I had for so many years;
My calmness returns, and I look forward to life; but
I always am asking why; and
It is clear that part of my drive is because
I must continue to search for an answer.

The Clock

The clock hangs there and stares at me
With hands that move no more.
Stopped when she died, and
When I thought my life had ended too.

It must be started again, or
At least put away out of sight.
It seems so simple, but
I try and I fail.

Recognition of when to back off
Is a lesson I have learned well.
Although, each obstacle must be faced,
Some can be postponed until tomorrow.

There is no standard time table
For grieving or healing.
Whatever I do must be normal, and
The correct thing for me.

The clock was her very special one,
Its not running is only a symbol,
Actually bothers nobody, and when I am ready,
The symbol will once again become just a clock.

The Louder I Ask Why

Even though time has passed,
I still ask why.
Time has made it easier; but
The louder I ask why,
The more silence there is.

Why am I here,
When she is gone?
I know that I had no say or no choice; but
The louder I ask why,
The more silence there is.

There must be a reason I can't find.
Her presence is with me,
She still guides me; and
The louder I ask why,
The more silence there is.

If she would not have been,
Then I would not be who I am.
I know the truth of this; but still
The louder I ask why,
The more silence there is.

What can I do but continue to reach out,
To take chances, to survive, to live, and
Wait for an answer; because
The louder I ask why,
The more silence there is.

Grief

During the grieving process (which in the case of a terminally ill loved one starts before the actual death), I've found there are times that I need to recall some things that hurt very severely. I particularly remember one time, along with all the swings of emotions that occurred during the last six months of Carol Ann's life, that was very devastating. Probably because of her pain, the results of the chemo treatments, her anguish over not being able to play the piano anymore, and the enormous number of pain pills prescribed, Carol Ann had a period of hallucination. She was so concerned that the inside-finish work on our home wouldn't be completed before she died that in her mind she was painting, wallpapering, driving nails, and cleaning up the mess. For four days she was absolutely frantic with activity even though bedfast.

During this time somebody had to be always by her side to help her with her work and prevent her from climbing out of bed. Our friends and I learned to go along with whatever she thought she had to do from throwing trash into an imaginary pit at the foot of her bed to mopping the walls.

One night, Jim and Vi were coming for a visit, and Vi was going to spend the night so I could get some sleep. Before they arrived, Roger and Marilyn stopped in. Carol Ann knew that Vi was going to spend the night, and she wanted the house spotless so that Vi wouldn't do anything except visit. Although there wasn't a speck of dirt anywhere, Carol Ann wanted me to mop the walls in the study where her hospital bed was. (We had put the bed there so Carol Ann could see outside to watch for the deer, foxes, birds, and our resident owl.)

As Roger, Marilyn, and I visited with Carol Ann, she kept telling me to mop the walls. I would explain that I was going to get it done before Vi arrived. Carol Ann insisted that it be done now and finally in a very disgusted voice told Marilyn that, since I wouldn't do the job, she would have to. About that time Jim and Vi arrived, and we also received a long-distance call from Judy, Carol Ann's best neighborhood friend from Fairborn, Ohio. I put Carol Ann on the phone and listened in on the portable phone so I could help remind her whom she was talking to.

The conversation went something like this: "Hi, Judy, how are your kids? How is Jim, and what have you been up to lately?— Now, Marilyn, I told you to get that wall mopped." (I reminded Carol Ann that she was talking to Judy.)

"Oh, that's right—I forgot. Hi, Judy, I thought you were Marilyn, and she won't get this wall mopped."

This cycle went on about six or seven times. Judy was laughing and crying on the other end of the phone conversation, I was trying to keep some resemblance of sanity on our end, and our company didn't know what to do except just be there. It hurt terribly to have to watch Carol Ann reduced to this level. But at the same time her actions were so funny that I couldn't help laughing while the tears flowed.

These hallucinations varied from seeing men looking in the windows until we would have our three dogs chase them away, to taking her glasses off when she didn't have them on, to talking to people in California that I didn't even know. After this constant four-day battle, Carol Ann finally got done with her work and wanted to be cleaned up. We washed her body all over for the longest time, and she finally said, "Don, please bring the dogs in. I want to tell them good-bye." I brought them to her bed one at a time. She petted each, gave instructions to take care of me, and then said good-bye. After that she was extremely quiet, didn't need pain pills, and seemed extremely peaceful. The next day she told me that I didn't have anything to worry about because Roxanne, Bandit, and

Pasha were puppies and so would never die and would always be there to take care of me. I still don't know why my heart didn't stop beating right then.

Each time I think I won't make it, I learn that survival is one of the strongest drives we humans have, and when I'm hurting, I must try to realize that I will make it to tomorrow or at least to the next hour and then to the next. Each step I take will make the next one a little easier, and I actually survive. At least so far.

Although there is no best time or place to have your loved one die, the night that Carol Ann died, she did have some of her loved ones by her side and she was where she wanted to be. It was so very important for both of us that she was at home and not in some hospital room. I knew that Saturday night that she was leaving this life, and I called her mother, her brother, and my mother to tell them to come. Fortunately, they were already on their way. They arrived just about twenty minutes before she actually died. Although very glad that she wasn't in pain any more, I could not believe it when she was really gone. All I wanted to do was talk about her. This need to keep her memory alive by talking about things we had done or places we had been has gone on and will continue doing so.

I remember one day after Carol Ann's death I needed to talk and absolutely nobody was available. I called my bereavement counselor with no luck. My mother was out with friends, my mother-in-law wasn't available, and my best friend and his wife were out of town. I actually started driving the streets looking for somebody I knew so I could talk. I don't think anybody can know devastation until he/she experiences the terrible loneliness of nobody, but I mean nobody, to talk to.

Late that night I finally reached Joan, a friend from my high school graduating class. Since she had lost her husband several years back, she understood what I was going through, and she just let me talk and cry, talk and cry. Finally I settled down. She helped me realize that only the passage of time would help take away the severe pain. She very tenderly said, "Don, I promise you, it will get better." That night I really found out how important it is to have somebody to talk to. I hope that in the future I will be able to return the compassion that has been shown to me.

Even recognizing how important it was and still is for me to talk about Carol Ann, there are other people who shared in her life who also needed the same opportunity.

When Vi, who is Jim's second wife, first met Carol Ann and me, she didn't really like Carol Ann. Of course, since Carol Ann, Jim, and I went back in our relationship over thirty-five years, Vi probably felt like an outsider.

One day, after Carol Ann's death, Vi had come out to my house to let my dogs out since I was to be gone all day. The next day Vi called me because she wanted to talk about Carol Ann. I went to their house, and Vi told me that, at first, she could not believe Carol Ann was as special or as caring as she appeared to be. Vi felt that it was a big front and after she realized it wasn't, Carol Ann became a very close friend. Vi was missing Carol Ann so much and was feeling jealous of Jim and me since we had known Carol Ann for over thirty years to her six. Vi told me that she had learned more from Carol Ann in those few years about loving, caring, and sharing than she had in the rest of her life.

Vi was really distraught and missed Carol Ann. Well, we shared a few stories, some laughs, lots of tears, and we did our best to understand that we had to rejoice in what we had shared with Carol Ann. Although Vi felt better after our conversation, and even though in the scheme of things I was healing by sharing these emotions with Vi, I did feel like my heart was breaking all over again. I thought I was going to die. Obviously I survived and now realize how important it was and still is for Carol Ann's loved ones to share and reach out to each other so that every one of us has a chance to survive our own personal grief.

Emotions versus Intellect

My life is in a turmoil;
My anchor has been lost.
Emotionally I doubt if I can make it,
Intellectually I know I must,
    And the battle goes on.

My friends try to help;
My family is very worried.
Emotionally everything I do seems to cause more pain,
Intellectually I know it should get better,
    And the battle goes on.

I try to stay busy,
But at times must be quiet and reflective.
Emotionally I can't make valid decisions.
Intellectually I have to take charge and go forward,
    And the battle goes on.

The traditions can't be the same;
I have problems trying to start new ones.
Emotionally I am tied to the past;
Intellectually I must plan for the future,
    And the battle goes on.

And the battle must continue,
For without the deep darkness of a moonless night,
How can one enjoy the beauty of the morning gentle light?
For without the bitter cold winter winds,
How can one love the warm spring breezes?
For without the pain of grief,
How can one return to the love of life?
    And, oh yes, the battle does go on.

During the process of grieving, there was one time when I think my emotions and body could not take any more of the pain and anguish, and my brain actually shut my feelings down and had me operating strictly on remote control for a period of about seven hours. I had been having extremely bad tension pain in my neck (although at the time I wasn't aware what it was), was irritable with my family and friends, not satisfied with anything I was doing, and no matter what I tried to do to relax, I became more and more distracted, while my emotional pain became worse and worse.

To this day I never have found out where I was that night or whom I was with, if anybody. I just know that I got out of my car in my garage. I did not remember really leaving my house but realized that the last time I was aware of anything I was at home at 6:00 or 7:00 P.M. It was now 1:30 A.M. I went into my house to find my answering machine blinking furiously and my three dogs standing with crossed legs, wanting desperately to go outside. I stood there feeling very strange, not knowing about the last seven hours.

I checked my phone messages, hoping that they might give me a clue to what I had been doing. My bereavement counselor was trying to locate me because I had called her, and the message I left her sounded extremely agitated. I checked my second message, and it was from a friend who I had called around 8:00 P.M. saying I was O.K., was in church, and would call back in a couple of hours. When I didn't call back in four or five hours, panic set in, and the message I got was to call no matter what time I got home. After touching base with everybody and settling myself down, I tried to remember where I had been, but it just never came back. Realizing that I had been driving around without knowing it scared me, and for the first time I really thought maybe I was going crazy and that I really wasn't going to survive this ordeal. But once again Carol Ann's presence and guidance prevailed. Although reluctantly, I did face the next day.

Even though the grieving process has been described as having different stages—anger, denial, sadness, pain, despair, insomnia, guilt, shock, crying, etc.—and these are well documented, I think each person handles his/her own grief a little differently. The one constant, that I have observed and specifically experienced myself, is that it is essential to share stories of your loved one's life. Even so, at times the pain is so severe during the telling that I have doubts.

But I've learned that the tears shed in private do not seem to be as healing as the shared ones—with a friend, a family member, or even a trained counselor. I guess I think everyone's grieving process is unique, and mine is right for me. It will help me not only to survive but eventually to choose a new kind of life. And, in the meantime, I will reach out to others, share the gifts I have left, and fully expect to find a satisfying, loved-filled life with another someday. I now firmly believe that I will, and I hope by sharing my feelings with you, will show that you can too.

When Does the Healing Start?

When does the healing start after the loss of a cherished loved one? I believe that it's after the pain is so severe that your very soul cries "No more, no more, no more." The scars that start to form are tender, subject to be reopened to let the anguish flow. Just when you believe that the tough covering will not let the pain return, something triggers the brain and starts the tears again. They tumble out like many unfulfilled dreams: plans for travel, starting the new phase of life, time to enjoy the bond with old friends have been dashed against the black rocks of reality.

You wonder if it is possible to reorganize your life to achieve any happiness. The help of old and new friends and the special care offered by your concerned family is bittersweet: beneficial, but external and short-lived.

As the first hour, the first day, and the succeeding weeks are gone, some things become easier, but some things constantly hurt. Each new first—the first month, the first anniversary (of your

marriage, of her birth or yours), the first Christmas celebration without her— brings chances to prove one really will survive, not because of what one does or doesn't do, but actually in spite of these things. As they say "Time will make things better."

The pain shows us we are alive and human, that the suffering is proportional to the loss of joy and happiness. But it's a constant battle. Fondly remembering the special love, we find the waves of sadness once more engulfing us; we miss that love. I guess this forces a decision between "I will never hurt this much again" or "I'll try to love again and make the rest of my life and somebody else's worthwhile."

To me, the choice has been very hard—and I guess it is for everybody. I am not looking for someone to take Carol Ann's place, and I am not in a hurry. But I now believe I will be able to love again and be loved someday. I think really it's the only possible choice for me, at least, the only one Carol Ann will approve, and that it is the only thing that Carol Ann would even demand I do.

Tunnel of Grief

It seems that just as the tunnel of grief gets the blackest, the light at the end brightens. Just as the pain gets the most severe, the promise of surviving is at its peak. The counteracting emotional forces—love/hate, joy/sadness, beauty/ugliness, giving/taking—constantly push my emotions to their outer limits. But even this constant ping-pong battle actually helps me because it shows me that I am alive and capable of feelings.

The numbness right after her death was probably necessary because they say severe emotional swings soon after loss can actually kill. But now that the numbness is gone, all the emotions of really living rush over me again in wave after wave after wave of highs and lows. In fact, sometimes both extremes are present, giving both joy and pain. The emotional roller-coaster ride even

makes some days very interesting, though causing me to wonder when stable Don will return.

I can now say the future looks promising if I can only survive the present. I know I am getting better but also that healing is a long-term process. But I can expect small recovery steps, and I believe daily activities will eventually become once more my warm friends.

Snow Gently Falling

The snow is gently falling and gradually covering the trees and ground with a brilliant white winter coat. The stark whiteness is a contrast to the dead brownness of late fall as the forest gets ready to sleep and prepare for spring. The seasons remind me so much of our life.

Our life together was like the never-ending spring and summer. At the start it was like the gentle warm spring. As our relationship became more serious and intense, the eventual merging of goals into marriage was as hot and happy as the never-ending summer days. Then, just when we were convinced that the summer joy would go on forever, the dreadful insidious disease struck. Just as sure as fall would arrive, cancer reached out and put us through the worst ordeal ever to face human beings.

Just as the deadness of the fall appearance has the brightness of oranges, reds, and yellows, the suffering and pain caused by that malignant growth brought us even closer together. This trial reinforced the very special love we had nurtured and allowed to grow to intense maturity. Her death and funeral drained me of all feeling for living or really caring about anything ever again. The drabness in my life was just like the dead appearance of the forest in late fall. My grief and pain slowly engulfed my emotions just as the snow covers the countryside and hides the dead brown appearance. The white covering, just like my severe pain, allows the living undercoat

to rest and regenerate in preparation for the coming gentle spring warmth. Just as surely as the snow will melt, my emotional stability will return and allow me to return to the living, caring world.

Winter seems extremely long, and my period of grief and recovery will seem as long and never ending. But, I know there is a new spring for me. It can never be the same; and, although a long time off, I believe that I am going to find a new, different, good sharing life and be able to be, once again, a functioning, caring human being.

To Trim the Tree: Should I or Shouldn't I?

The Christmas holiday approaches;
The presents need to be bought;
The families prepare to come home;
And the tree awaits.
    Should I or
        Shouldn't I?

The box of ornaments sits and waits;
The lights need to be checked;
The garland should be unraveled;
And the tree awaits.
    Should I or
        Shouldn't I?

The plans for parties are made;
The cards are addressed;
The turkey has been ordered;
And the tree awaits.
    Should I or
        Shouldn't I?

Should I?
> Only if it helps me.

Shouldn't I?
> Only if it hurts too much.

Should I?
> Only if I want to.

Shouldn't I?
> Only if I don't want to.

And the tree awaits.
> Will or won't I?
> I will if it is right and if I feel that it is.

What Is of Value?

What is of value?
> Profession?
> Pets?
> Achievements?

What is of value?
> Possessions?
> Friends?
> Family?

What is of value?
> Sharing the trust of a best friend?
> Giving oneself to others?
> The special love of one's life?

When some of these things and all the rest are in one person and that person is taken away, what then?
> WHAT THEN????

Return '90

Where is the person I was before her death?
Who is this new man I've become?
Why can't I be as I was?
When will I return?

What, Where, Who, Why, and When?
I try to push up from my pain and grief,
But I fail.
I know I am different and I don't want to be.

I want what I had,
But I can't go back,
My future is far beyond my reach.
I must learn to accept the now as it comes and goes.

The pain is severe, but I manage.
My life will be different, but still it will be mine.
Plans will be on hold for a while.
I must reach out for help and to help.

So, dear ones,
    Care for me,
      Comfort me,
        Understand my pain,
          Try to know I don't know who I am now.
          I promise, the one I was will return.

Time Must Do the Healing

Since the severe pain has subsided,
The depths of the jabs of despair surprise me:
Doing laundry devastates me;
Fixing breakfast puts me in a blue funk.
Time must do the healing.

The angry storms beat me unmercifully,
And my anchor has been viciously ripped away;
When I do what I want, I hurt somebody else;
What I believe is best for somebody else causes me anxiety.
Time must do the healing.

Becoming a recluse would surely kill me;
Reaching out, although necessary, gives chance of mistakes;
Even though mistakes are what we learn from,
They drain energy excessively.
Time must do the healing.

Oh yes, time must do the healing
Although time can't bring you back.
It gives me a chance to recover;
It gives me new challenges;
It gives me new opportunities;
It gives me new friends; and
It may give me a second chance to find happiness with someone
    new, someday.

Once More

Once more severe pain has returned;
Once more my loss overwhelms me;
Once more I was tested;
Once more my family stood by me;
Once more my friends rallied to my side;
Once more my counselor listened and helped,
And once more I survived.

Surviving this current crisis has taught me much:
I can say I really know I will survive;
I know that the severe pain may come back;
I also know that the pain will not destroy me.
Although I am battered and hurt,
I must go forward;
Although emotionally I am completely drained and exhausted,
I must trust my decisions and not second-guess so much.

Once more the pain and despair proved I am alive;
Once more I realized that I am not emotionally dead;
Once more I faced the blast furnace of life;
Once more my roller-coaster ride has stabilized;
Once more the future does not look so dark;
Once more I can try to share,
And once more I survived and will reach out,
Oh yes, once more.

Obstacles

Time can be healing,
But also very frustrating.
I want to be well and strong now,
But I know I can't rush this journey.

The pain and anguish can't be avoided;
The passage goes through obstacles;
To sidestep them today
Will make them harder tomorrow.

Facing each fear and each pain
Makes me stronger;
As long as I allow myself time
To back off when I must.

Some problems need dissecting
And changed to smaller hurdles;
What can't be cleared in one huge jump
Can be traversed one small step at a time.

The Fog

The thick chilling fog rolls in;
Usual landmarks are instantly obscured;
I know that the road is there,
But it is also hidden.

I slowly move, feel, and stumble;
Each obstacle seems gigantic in the deep fog;
I back up, start again, and find another wall;
Frustration sets in as the fog becomes even thicker.

The swirling winds briefly push the fog away;
I see an opening to the sunlight,
And then the fog engulfs me once more;
I wonder if I will ever see clearly again.

Spring

Spring is not too far away;
I feel it in the air,
Sense it with the smell of the forest,
And see it in the first new growth.

Spring breezes will take away the chill in my soul;
Bright sunlight will warm my outlook;
With each new spring day I will get better,
But I must be aware of memories of that approaching summer night.

With help I will make it past June 16th;
On that day I will need extra support;
Good memories must be drawn upon,
To assure that I will survive my ordeal.

One More Day

The sun slowly vanishes;
Another night is upon me;
Activities fill the time,
And I have faced one more day.

My life is becoming better.
The quiet times do not bother me so much;
I am carefully making this house my home,
And I have faced one more day.

Although I am becoming emotionally stable,
There are still some lows;
The severe pain reappears occasionally,
And I have faced one more day.

I believe that I will survive my ordeal,
But there are still hurdles to clear,
So very carefully I will do so,
And, oh yes, I have faced one more day.

Desert Winds

Nine months is short,
But a new life grows in that time;
Grieving and healing take much longer,
To adjust to my life without her may take an eternity.

Each day is like a speck of sand:
The wind blows it here and there,
And many times there is no rest
Because changes are scary but required.

Even the vastness of a desert
Is mercifully broken by an occasional oasis;
The water is clear and refreshing
While the shade cools the fevered brow.

This weary traveler needs to rest,
Let the angry hot desert winds blow,
Reflect on life,
And allow the present to happen.

Too Big of a Price to Pay

My creative drive is rampant, and
I can't stop the flow of words.
It seems that I am just an instrument
Released by your death.
And it is too big of a price to pay.

Am I possessed by your creative spirit?
Where do these thoughts come from?
I hear a song you loved, and
The smile appears, the tears flow, and the words tumble out.
And it is too big of a price to pay.

Our love was special;
It knew no limits or bounds.
It is still with me and must be shared.
Because, you told me "don't be alone."
And it is too big of a price to pay.

I have no choice but to go forward,
Because you would demand that I do.
Maybe my words will help people remember,
You were real,
    You were honest,
        You were loved, and
           You are sorely missed.
              And, oh yes,
                  It is too big of a price to pay.

Heads or Tails

The sounds,
    The smells,
        The vibrations,
Once more, the ghosts have returned.

I see her suffering,
I hear her cry out,
I want to stop remembering the pain, and
Recall only the joy and happiness.

Where will the next jab come from?
What is the cause of this regression?
Why can't I get past this day,
Without this knot around my heart?

My good memories are comforting, but
The bad ones are so vivid and last too long.
Do I really remember pain more
Than the beauty of our shared love?

Do I need the hurt
To treasure the joy?
I guess without tails
There would be no heads!

Fear

Murky fingers enclose my mind, heart, and soul.
Blackness clouds my judgment;
Some decisions work out wrong;
Fear may be my worst enemy yet.

Is emotional suicide starting?
I have hurt some people I care about;
Panic is showing up;
Fear may be my worst enemy yet.

My emotional strength is slowly being eroded;
What can my next move be?
What is driving me?
Fear may be my worst enemy yet.

I need my friends to rally around me,
But I believe that my actions have hurt too much,
Can time make very much of a difference?
Oh yes, fear may be my worst enemy yet.

But

Waves of anxiety cover my life;
Fear cascades around me;
The loss hurts,
But how else could it be?

I must draw on my strengths
And count on my very special friends;
The sharing will make the time go by,
But will it be enough?

The last year has been a century long,
Though it seems like only yesterday she was still here;
Now is the time to find a safe haven,
But where can it lead?

I don't know what I want;
I can't tell what I need;
I am hurt, scared, and desperate.
But all this will also pass!

?

As I went through this very difficult, long grieving process, I started needing to reach out and trying to have some kind of life without the physical presence of my loved one. Everything I did with new or old friends in my now very active single life gave me both temporary joy and also at times very severe pain. There were times, even when I just had dinner out with a family that knew both Carol Ann and me, that I felt very guilty. Although I was not doing anything wrong, these guilty feelings rose because she wasn't along to enjoy the good times with good friends. If I had not recognized that these feelings were normal, I would have thought I was actually going crazy. Maybe indeed that part of the grieving process is a type of craziness. With time I have noticed that these guilty feeling are becoming less severe even though I constantly miss Carol Ann and still sometimes question why she was taken away from me.

The Journey

Where will this path take me?
If I really knew, would I choose left or right?
The final destination may not be that important,
But experiencing each emotion during the journey is
   essential.

As I continued expanding my life without her, my emotional decision-making capability was tested. Although it is very natural to want exactly what I had, it is not possible to find it, even though

I was intellectually convinced that I wasn't really looking for a replacement for Carol Ann. Emotionally, and most of the time without even being aware of it, I probably compared potential relationships with what I had for over thirty years with Carol Ann. Since I wasn't aware of this, there were times that this caused undue pressure on my newly formed friendships and actually did end the chance of anything special happening and, for sure, anything lasting.

During these very trying times, I had to learn to build the basis for a strong friendship first; then the more intense emotional connection, if it was going to occur, would at least give me a chance to experience love once again. To make it even more difficult during this time, and probably because subconsciously I couldn't imagine experiencing the pain of losing a special loved one again, I built a wall of resistance that would not allow me to let anybody get close. I particularly would not allow myself to admit that I was really caring about a person. This situation of looking for something special with one person and at the same time being afraid of allowing that to happen caused me some very difficult—though interesting—emotional times.

I have noticed that others too experience the need to frantically fill every possible minute with busy activity. There were times that—if I didn't have something planned for every night of the week by the preceding Sunday—I would become hyper, worried, and extremely concerned about whom I was going to call or what I was going to do. This need, although apparently at times looking destructive to others, I believe is very important to at least some grieving people. I guess, since it is impossible to disconnect one's brain, one tries to get so busy that he doesn't have time to really think about what he has lost, what he misses so very much, and wonders if he is going to survive. This type of action, at least in my case, seemed the only way to handle the despair, the severe pain, and the very real need to share feelings with other people. I ended up joining three singles groups, volunteering to take on responsibilities in all of them. Soon I began wondering why—when the activities of the groups and the other friendships I was trying to handle started overlapping—I felt as if I was having a nervous breakdown!

I found out the hard way that the problem with this frantic activity is that there were times that I pushed myself into situations that I wasn't ready to handle. My emotional fibers were so raw from my loss that I started doubting every decision I made. Eventually this frantic activity did lessen, and I accepted the fact that I needed to relax when I could and let time do its healing. I will admit that I had the hardest time doing this and continually pushed myself too hard, even though many of my friends and family recognized what I was doing and tried to tell me so. It was very difficult for me to admit that I was actually running from my pain and was trying to hide. Fortunately I did finally listen to my friends, family, and my bereavement counselor and started to slow down. The writing of this book was the best therapy.

Giving

Giving is sometimes achieved by taking;
Taking comfort allows a person to give;
Asking for help is scary and exposes frailties;
Transition from care-giving to care-taking is difficult,
But to survive I must learn that giving goes two ways.

Since this section is actually about what I don't have the capability or really the desire to know—basically what does the future hold after I have gone through love, death, and grief—I can only share what I feel. I know that I am getting better each day. I have had some very rough days, and I know that I will have some more. I also know that the pain is not going to destroy me, and I am convinced that when the time is right I will find someone to share the rest of my life with. I also know that we will be able to give each other friendship, companionship, love, and passion. That time will come, and then the question mark will disappear.

When will this happen? I don't know.
When will the pain stop? I don't know.
When will I really enjoy life again? I don't know.
Why does life seem so unfair sometimes?
I do know that life is not unfair; life is just life.
I do know that the pain will not win.
I do know that I will survive.
I do know that I look forward now.
I do know that you can too.

The only advice I leave you is to feel, reach out to others and share; create if you can, try to let time do its healing job, and believe that you will survive.

Reach Out

The pain is unbearable;
Anxiety rolls in on giant waves;
Survival does not seem achievable,
But they say I must reach out.

Simple tasks are hard,
Hard ones impossible;
Clear thoughts just don't come,
But they say I must reach out.

The void she left cannot be filled;
Business fills the hours but frustrates,
Suffering is my constant companion;
But they say I must reach out.

They say by reaching out,
    I will find that I am not alone,
    My strength will return,
        I can survive;
            I can share my pain, and
                I will gain control of my life.

They say by reaching out,
    I receive help, compassion, and friendship,
    And someday, when the pain is less severe,
        I will be able to help somebody else because
        I will care.

Letting Go

How do I really say good-bye?
What will stop this pain of missing you?
I know life must go on;
Oh, how and when can I let go?

Anger's icy fingers grip my very soul;
I am mad at my desire to find some happiness;
New friends cause both joy and pain;
Oh, how and when can I let go?

Guilt is constant.
I know it should not be.
You told me to live, enjoy; if possible love again!
Oh, how and when can I let go?

But I don't need to let you go,
To give you up,
To be guilty.
Our life is done but always ours;
Death has divided my life:
    With you and
        Without you.

With you, I shared a very special love.
Without you,
    I must build again,
      Make new friends,
        Maybe even share and care again,
          And all because of you.

Choices

The choices are many and varied,
Necessity for making them circles like vultures.
There are no easy answers
And thousands of difficult questions:
Choices, Choices, Choices.

Intellectual choices are simple,
Emotional ones impossible;
My bridge between them is gone;
Problem-solving techniques are useless:
Choices, Choices, Choices.

I hope as I recover to do better.
What decisions I make affect others;
Concern for them at times confuses me;
Sometimes no decision is the best:
Choices, Choices, Choices.

I must rely on gut reactions.
My past is the only strong guide I have.
As my emotions recover, I will get stronger;
Decisions will be become easier and I hope correct:
Choices, Choices, Choices.

What can I do but try?
What can I expect but the best?
What will happen will happen,
So, I choose what I feel is right;
    But I delay things when I am not sure;
      I must allow time for healing and
        Not make wrong choices because of my pain.

Accept What Can Be

Emotionally I was alone and desperate because
My soul mate had been taken away.
I was afraid because I didn't know who I was.
Every place I went I looked for her, and
I searched for her presence in everybody I met.

The path through the despair was filled with frantic activity
While I reached out to share but also drew back in fear.
Living and reaching out was so very scary,
But hiding to be safe was a desperate devastation of its own.
I had to learn to rejoice in what had been and
    accept what can be.

Without Them

They say time has a way of healing, but
I wonder if the scars are ever permanently hard.
Sometimes even good memories reopen wounds.
I miss what we had, want what we had, and
I look for what we had.
Achieving the same thing is impossible.
Intellectually I know this, but
Emotionally it is hard to accept.

Neither the good times nor the tough times
Can be the same.
The players are different, and
Even though living is the script,
The sub-plots are all changed.
Making new friends and facing new experiences
Are necessary, but sometimes scary, and
Without them, I would surely wither and die.

Counter Balance

Why is there so much pain?
The cry of a hungry child,
The anguish of a grieving spouse, and
The lament of the abandoned lover
Echo around me.

Must there be pain to appreciate joy?
The laughter of a happy child,
The songs of the musicians, and
The lyrics of the poets
Surround my senses.

Would only happiness and joy become boring?
Cries and laughter must coexist,
Anguish and songs are required, and
Laments and lyrics are necessary
For me to make comparisons.

I see somebody else's pain and I feel it in my heart.
I witness love and my soul is renewed.
I share the anguish of a friend and I hope I have helped.
I listen, try to understand, and grow because I care.
    Must there be pain?
        I guess it is another question with no answer.

This Weary Man

Take away the indecisions;
Make the uncertainties go away;
Let me have some peace;
This weary man needs rest.

Her presence is everywhere;
I rejoice in the good memories,
But at times they become burdens;
This weary man needs rest.

I know that there will be somebody else special someday,
And my impatience is bothersome;
Desire for living today cannot be wrong.
This weary man needs rest.

Why must the past and present collide so violently?
The past is over; the present is a stepping stone to the future.
I must find new strengths;
Oh yes, this weary man needs rest.

What Now?

My resolve was severely tested.
I found myself failing my own criteria,
Am I not as strong as I thought?
Will I survive this trauma?

I cannot go back;
While going forward is frightening,
And standing still is frustrating,
I must dig in deeper and hold on tighter.

Weighing all the factors is mind-boggling.
Intellectual planning may not be the answer;
Emotional happiness seems unreachable,
But maybe it is really too soon.

When Will the Darkness Change?

The rain continues to fall;
Darkness encloses the countryside;
It seems as if the sunshine has completely disappeared;
The brilliant blue sky must be up there someplace.
When will the darkness change?

The stark trees show no signs of life;
Dead leaves cover the ground;
It seems that life has totally left;
The spring warmth has to return.
When will the darkness change?

I know that the darkness has to change.
Just as the long winter will end,
Just as the gentle spring warm breezes will arrive,
Just as surely as the trees will turn green again,
Life has not left;
   It is only
     Resting,
       Allowing time for recovery,
         Waiting for new growth.

Even though very difficult to do, I have to wait for new life
   to form and flourish in the bright sun.
Oh yes, I must believe that the darkness will change.

Enough Time

Black clouds boil and cover the horizon;
Darkness blots out the bright sun;
Emotional needs drive me;
My mind has a difficult time coping;
Once again I have pushed myself too hard.

The joy of my past slams into my present;
I want to replace what I had,
But it is too soon to make valid decisions,
While indecision causes confusion and pain;
Once again I have pushed myself too hard.

I feel that what I give is not enough;
My needs are hard to define;
If one special person is my need,
Why does my past deny the capability to achieve it?
Once again I have pushed myself too hard.

When I get close to those special feelings,
Panic overpowers me,
Fear chills my raw emotions,
And I seek frantic activity.
Once again I have pushed myself too hard.

What do I back off from?
Where do I turn?
Time may be an ally,
But how much time is enough?
Although causing casualties, it seems,
   I need to push myself,
     To push myself,
        To push myself.

I Must Learn

Every emotional fiber end is raw,
My stabilizer must be inoperative,
Where has the constant guidance gone?
Have my needs changed that much?
Or am I trying to heal too fast?

It seems as if part of me has been violently removed,
My desire for only one relationship remains,
But, my capability for accepting it has died and been buried.
Why can't I be happy with what I find
And stop looking for something different or something more?

I don't recognize the difference between my past and my present,
The ties to my past cause both good memories and deep pain,
The joy of the present collides with my past and hurts.
While in this confusion, whom do I trust?
My emotions overpower me while my intellect tries to counsel.

To just enjoy what comes my way may be easy.
I just want to be me, but I don't know who that is anymore,
I give everything I have, but in my mind that isn't enough.
Where, oh, where is the missing piece to the puzzle?
How can I solve the mystery while the fog is so thick?

I must learn to just accept what is freely given;
I must learn to realize that I give what I can;
I must learn to let happen what happens;
I must learn to not push myself so hard;
Oh yes, I must learn.

My Two Lives

Will this void ever be filled again?
Only time will tell.
I try not to compare the present with my past,
But how can I not compare this to such great happiness?

My life's yardstick is mostly our journey,
Each step ingrained in my memory;
Everything I do reminds me,
And I smile, but I also hurt.

I have no choice but to go forward,
Although I know that looking back is essential.
My two lives must coexist,
And I will build something good on my past.

That Has to Be Enough

I look but don't want to see;
I ask but don't want to hear;
My past still controls my present
While my present blocks the future.

Everywhere I go our memories are there;
Everything I do we did.
To build a new life seems impossible
Because the old life is what I want.

Surviving today
Should make tomorrow better.
Every small step taken
Can only add to that first mile traveled.

Maybe I really expect too much of myself;
Changes in my life have been drastic;
I feel that I am getting better while trying to go forward;
And maybe, for now, that has to be enough.

Help

What can be will vanish,
Into what could have been,
If we are afraid to take chances,
Or over-analyze every emotion.

Soundness of decisions,
Can only be proved in the future,
And not trying is more of a loss,
Than reaching out and failing.

To miss new friendships,
Is a loss that can't be retrieved,
Second chances are very rare,
And if appearing must be grasped and held.

Whatever happens,
   Helps me grow,
     Heal,
        Survive,
          And will help me live.

Kaleidoscope

The bright colors crash together:
Different shapes form, change, and collide.
The memories of our past
Join with my present
And, together, cause joy and concern.

Merging of what I was and what I am
Can be stressful,
But can also be exciting.
My two lives must become friends
And not fight each other.

The key is in the operator of the kaleidoscope;
The jagged shapes and constant changes
Are mainly caused by the viewer
And not by the scenes' acting on the viewer,
So I must take control of the inputs.

Look to the Future

I am alone but not lonely.
I have much to be thankful for,
Which I must share;
To grow I must give of myself.

The grief, pain, and tears have made me strong.
My suffering has not been wasted;
Despair's dark tunnel has been traveled,
The depths of hell withstood.

What will the future hold?
What distant vision clarify?
Can I help my healing?
What can I expect of myself?

My battered soul is intact;
My heart, although badly bent, did not break;
My brain, though greatly strained, still works;
My emotions, although bloody, are healthy.

So, Don, look to the future,
Things that need doing,
New friends to enjoy,
Family for sharing,
New challenges,
Oh yes, Don, look to the future.

A New Year

A new year has arrived,
The time for self-evaluation;
My guidance must come from within;
What will the new year bring?

My emotions are still raw and need time to heal,
But it is time to challenge my brain;
Plans need to be formed;
What will the new year bring?

I know any new start is scary;
Taking chances is tough but thrilling;
I must go forward, even if very slowly.
What will the new year bring?

Although disconcerted I happily greet the new year.
Whatever the new year brings,
   I am ready
     To take chances,
       To experience life again.

I Welcome

The fog of despair is being lifted;
The heart-breaking pain, though constant, is now a dull ache,
I believe I am getting better, and
I welcome health.

It's finally started;
My loss is still as great, but
The covering scars are forming, and
I welcome them.

Choices are mine to make;
My emotions, although still tied to the past, are now less loud,
I make decisions now, even
Welcome them.

Christmas has come and been celebrated;
I have reminisced and hurt;
I have laughed and cried, and
I welcome life.

The tears flow gently now;
The thoughts of her pain are not so prevalent now.
Our years of love and sharing care for me, and
I welcome them.

I welcome the sunrise,
    The moon-lit nights,
      New friends,
        Closeness of shared compassion,
          Some of the old Don,
            And the chance to live again.

I Am Surviving

I have come through the severe pain;
I have come up from the depths of despair;
The days are still at times extremely difficult;
The nights are still long and restless,
But, I am surviving.

Each new day presents a different challenge;
Each first makes me stronger;
My tears still fall at the strangest times;
My pain, although less severe, prods me periodically,
But, I am surviving.

My future does look promising;
My past will be my strength.
There may be emotional regression;
There will be times I will ask for help;
But, I am surviving.

I have self-healing to accomplish;
I have plans for creating things;
I have sharing to do;
I have a lot of living to do.
Oh yes, I will survive.

The Rest of My Life

As I travel my personal road to recovery,
My constant companions, Suffering and Pain, are less severe.
As I avoid the deepest potholes of despair,
I need to reach out to my friends and loved ones.

As each mile is slowly covered,
New experiences help the healing process;
As I stop at each roadside rest area,
My battered emotions get a little stronger.

As I share life's events and try to give of myself,
My self-assurance returns;
As I relearn my skills in communication,
The doubts are becoming fewer.

As I reach out both to give and take,
Fresh healing growth covers the raw wounds of grief;
As I realize how much I have left to share,
The possibilities of the future are very exciting.

As the trip becomes less hectic
And the good times outnumber the bad,
My healing does occur more and more,
And the jabs of severe pain do diminish.

As the pace of frantic activity lessens,
My old demeanor slowly returns.
Because I know that I am getting better
And that my trip through life will be special.
Oh yes, I know that the rest of my life will be special.

Epilogue

As you can tell from reading this book, I am a very positive person who believes that life is good and that I expect the best from it. Of course, before Carol Ann's sickness and death, I had never had any devastating losses or severe problems in my life. Losing her has reinforced my belief that life is short and very precious. I also don't want to ever look back and say if I had only done this or tried that or shared something of importance with a friend. . . .

I will admit that during this past year I have been a very difficult person to be associated with. There were times when I didn't recognize myself, didn't handle personal relationships very well, pushed myself too hard, made some very big mistakes, and tried too hard to cure my own grieving pain. I eventually learned that I wasn't Superman, that I needed to reach out for help, and most of all that only after a long time will the pain, although never gone, not hurt so much that I will be able to find someone else to share my life and love.

The most important thing I learned was that I am very fortunate to be able to write and get my many different emotions out to share with friends and loved ones. I hope sharing them with you will make your grieving process easier, and if some good comes from this, maybe Carol Ann's death will not have been such a complete loss.

By

By reaching out,
We share, we learn, and we grow,
By helping,
We heal, we become stronger, we survive, and we live.

In a Flash

The light was green.
Traffic moved.
Squealing tires and burning rubber!
The semi could not stop.
In a flash, I once again realized life is so very precious.

Reaction, avoidance, and no panic.
Brake hard and turn right.
Semi slides by!
My heartbeat pounds in my ears.
In a flash I know what must be done.

I must write,
    I must create,
      I must share,
        I must publish the book.
In a flash, the gauntlet has been thrown and retrieved.
    In a flash, I know!

Create

Severe pain and overpowering joy.
They exist together.
The conflict is difficult, but
Without both, I could not survive.

I receive, I give, and I create.
My mind is on fire.
My thoughts pour out.
Words, phrases, and sentences grow.

Where does all this energy come from?
Do I really have a choice?
   I must write,
     I must write,
       I MUST CREATE.

A Chill Crosses My Shoulders

Evening temperatures are a little cooler.
The first sign of leaves changing their color
Makes me wonder where has this year gone, and
A chill crosses my shoulders.

Time is such a precious commodity.
It must be used wisely, because
I don't know about tomorrow, and
A chill crosses my shoulders.

Friendships started today
May not exist tomorrow.
This causes me sadness, and
A chill crosses my shoulders.

What we do today
Becomes our memories for tomorrow.
Even though I think this is good,
A chill crosses my shoulders.

But wait, this chill that crosses my shoulders,
Is only the uncertainty of my tomorrow.
And, tomorrow is mine for the taking,
But only after I experience today.

Time to Believe

The fragile plants extend their roots,
While they need sunlight, water, and food.
They grow stronger and reach out, but
Adversity is everywhere.

Mother Nature is, at times, very harsh.
The wind bends their stalks,
Rain pelts them unmercifully, and
Insects try to devour them.

Although some are destroyed,
Most survive and continue growing.
Finally, blooms appear, and
Their beauty is breathtaking.

How did some survive and others not?
The sunlight was the same,
The water was the same, and
The food was the same.

Physical dimensions are not all that matters,
Believing in the future is required.
Enjoying today's beauty as growth for tomorrow occurs,
Gives enough time to really believe.

Today Is Yesterday's Tomorrow

As the minutes build to hours,
We have gone from the past to the present,
Are anticipating the future, and realize that
Today is yesterday's tomorrow.

Although none of us can know what will happen,
We must look forward with confidence and joy.
To allow the past to cloud our vision might make us forget that
Today is yesterday's tomorrow.

Each beauty we see and enjoy, and
Each person we reach out to in friendship
Would not have occurred if we had forgotten that
Today is yesterday's tomorrow.

To fear tomorrow because of the heartbreaks of yesterday
Can only diminish what we can experience today, and
Then tomorrow becomes less, because
Today is yesterday's tomorrow.

So my fellow travelers through time;
Reach out, enjoy life, anticipate tomorrow, and remember that
Although we always exist in today,
Today is yesterday's tomorrow.

A Message from the Other Side of Pain

The delicate blooms of the dogwood,
The deep green fir trees, and
The gentle evening breezes are
Difficult to appreciate,
While the voice of my soul
Is crying from the other side of pain.

My eyes need to see beauty,
My ears need to hear music, and
My heart needs to feel love, but
Many barriers block them,
While the voice of my soul
Is crying from the other side of pain.

I lift myself up from the ashes of grief,
I force myself up from the depths of despair,
My bloody emotions scream to be well, and
The wall of silence is broken
By the voice of my soul
Crying from the other side of pain.

As beauty returns to my life,
As music again soothes my ears, and
As once again I have learned to love,
My emotions have been strengthened
By the voice of my soul sending
A message from the other side of pain.

The next three poems are important because they specifically show that I was trying to reach out and help other people, which was good therapy and helped me to realize that my life would go forward.

Life

(This poem was for and given to a couple in which the wife, who was a cancer patient of the same doctor that Carol Ann had, miscarried their first child. They wanted a baby so badly and had a hard time deciding whether to try or not after her cancer had been declared in remission.)

The flower of the special union did not survive;
The possibilities of the new life will not occur.
What will result from this loss?
What will replace this void?
How very unfair life seems to be.

The love that formed this chance must sustain them;
The caring times must be extra special now;
What has happened can not be changed;
What could have been need not be forgotten.
How very unfair life seems to be.

The time was not right;
The decision to try again has to be made;
What occurred may again occur;
What plans were formed must be formed again.
How very unfair life seems to be.

The importance of sharing love is paramount;
The union of life, body, and soul cannot be denied;
What we give freely returns tenfold;
What could be only occurs if we don't stop trying.
How very unfair life seems to be.

When we survive our trials,
When we overcome life's pain and despair,
When we always try our best,
When we share life's setbacks,
We prove that although seemingly unfair,
    Life is what makes us what we are;
      Life is what forms us humans;
        Life is not unfair;
          Life is just life.

Surviving
(This poem was written to my grieving-support group.)

The cause of our pain is obvious:
We think that the void in our lives can't ever be filled again;
But we must reach out and share.
Each story is unique and special,
And the memories will sustain us.

As we travel our separate, difficult, healing journeys,
Our emotional paths will cross and entwine;
My grief is mine alone,
But it does make me understand yours,
And the sharing will sustain us.

The things I can't do yet
Sound much like some of yours;
The sleepless nights come and go.
We must believe that it will get better,
And our mutual caring will sustain us.

So, my kindred grieving souls,
Remember your loved one and rejoice in what you had;
Share your feelings with all of us;
Accept care from family, friends, and loved ones,
Because we can help each other survive.

Days, Weeks, and Months
(This poem was written to my grieving-support group.)

I wonder what time will bring;
Each day has the chance for learning;
Our paths touch many lives;
We relate, take, and give a bit of ourselves,
And one more day has been faced.

Concern for each other makes us strong.
As we share our pain, our fears, and our joy,
We learn that survival is possible,
But it is obvious that grieving is hard work,
And one more day has been faced.

We reach out and help when we can;
A gentle word of understanding quiets despair;
An unexpected favor saves one more hour
While a hug warms the heart,
And one more day has been faced.

Yes, one more day has been faced,
And because each day turns into weeks and then months,
   We survive,
    Go forward,
     Learn to live again,
      And someday the pain will not be severe anymore.